Angela Hume's profoundly intimate collection imagines how the porous interiors of women's bodies are harmed and sickened by sexual violence, the industrial food system, racist fascism, climate change, and environmental contamination. In the middle of everything, Hume rehearses acts of tenderness, empathy, courage, and desire in order to protect and "love the body in its / one life its singular intensity after all."
— Craig Santos Perez, author of *Habitat Threshold*

This is poetry about the vast, interlocking systems of capitalism, agriculture, fossil fuels, genetic engineering, patriarchy, heteronormativity, settler colonialism, and white supremacy. This is poetry that declares "the truth is not / new but still // mostly very / difficult to face." This is poetry that asks, "what is poetry but / a bloc // a collective self- / defense act"? This poetry is indeed a powerful counter to our death- and profit-driven culture, which harnesses our bodily and psychic desires with food and commodities and societal structures that do us profound damage and cannot nourish us. This is poetry that commands us instead to "love the body in its / one life its singular intensity after all." And it is a love song to the "profound intimacy / of a material world" in which we find ourselves, together. Thank you Angela Hume for facing truth. We have never needed this music more.
— Brian Teare, author of *Doomstead Days*

Written between fires and uprisings, the Pacific coast and "shelf stable" midwest, *Interventions for Women* aches. In the long title poem, Hume performs a kind of gene sequence on the violence of white girlhood as it is built into the DNA of climate change: agrobusiness, surveillance, sexual violence, "settler / colonial eating." Connecting food insecurity to disordered eating to forms of mutual care and collective resistance, these poems place themselves in the debt of earlier feminisms. It is no mistake the book begins with a prayer of galactic biological dimension and reaches towards new sequences of relationality: "love is a cord and / all love is political."
— Stephanie Young, author of *Pet Sounds*

interventions for women

previous works

full-length book

Middle Time (Omnidawn, 2016)

poetry chapbooks

Meat Habitats (DoubleCross Press, 2019)
Melos (Projective Industries, 2015)
The Middle (Omnidawn, 2013)
Second Story of Your Body (Portable Press at Yo-Yo Labs, 2011)

interventions for women

angela hume

OMNIDAWN PUBLISHING

OAKLAND, CALIFORNIA

2021

Cover image credit: "In Vitro Meat Habitat." Mitchell Joachim, Terreform ONE.

Text set in Electra LT Std

Cover design by adam b. bohannon

Library of Congress Cataloging-in-Publication Data

Names: Hume, Angela, author.
Title: Interventions for women / Angela Hume.
Description: Oakland, California : Omnidawn Publishing, 2021. | Includes
  bibliographical references. | Summary: "Were you raised to be a girl?
  The kind of girl who grows up to become a woman? Were you shamed for
  being not girl enough or too much girl? Were you looked at, talked over,
  touched, fed, psychiatrized, or indoctrinated in ways you didn't want to
  be or didn't understand? Were you told that if you'd just smile and try
  to be happy, everything would be better? At a certain point, did you
  look around and start to see how big the system is that holds you, a
  system that wants to use you up, along with everyone and everything
  around you? Did you start to see how it uses you in order to use others,
  and how you suffer as a consequence of that use while also benefiting
  from it? Did you start to see how complicit you are in every part of it?
  Are you sick, grieving, furious, on fire? Did you answer yes to some of
  these questions? To none of them? Then this book is for you. I wrote
  this book for you."-- Provided by publisher.
Identifiers: LCCN 2021034559 | ISBN 9781632430960 (paperback)
Subjects: LCSH: Women--Poetry. | LCGFT: Poetry.
Classification: LCC PS3608.U438 I58 2021 | DDC 811/.6--dc23
LC record available at https://lccn.loc.gov/2021034559

Published by Omnidawn Publishing, Oakland, California
www.omnidawn.com   (510) 237-5472
10 9 8 7 6 5 4 3 2 1
ISBN: 978-1-63243-096-0

contents

may the human animals   9

interventions for women   17

drowning effects   65

you were there   85

meat habitats   99

say no   125

notes   139

acknowledgements   147

may the human animals

Minneapolis, Minnesota, 2019.

I borrowed some of the language here from the September 2019 *IPCC Special Report: Global Warming of 1.5 °C*, the May 2019 *IPBES Global Assessment Report on Biodiversity*, and various writings on depression and human empathy.

learn new skills by imitation

fire the neuron when the action

is performed   and also when

the action is observed in another

thus mirroring the behavior

of that other   reach net zero global

anthropogenic CO_2 emissions

stop the earth from receiving

incoming energy from the plasma

core radiating 4.26 million

metric tons per second   more

energy than the earth itself radiates

into space   brighter disk   limb

darkening   only the cooler layers

that produce less light can be seen

may the human animals

facilitate helping behaviors

stop the hoarding of food supplies

medicine   the caging and modification

of human and other animals

stop the CO2 from soaking the reef

and also the worldwide

reduction of a pH balance that

marine calcifiers need to build

skeletons shells corrals crustaceans

snails   even light-harvesting algae

encase themselves in carbonate platelets

radial   continuous   basket-shaped

disc-shaped wishbone-shaped

rhombohedral   the colors of

moss and tea   may the human animals

redistribute across populations

change lifestyles to enable adaptation

fathom the relief of an earth without them

imagine another human animal's

thoughts and feelings from that

other's point of view instead of from

their own   may the human animals say

i am here   i know what you are feeling

is real   your life is important to me

and you are not alone

tunnel through a seemingly hardened

crust to the warm wet electrochemical

center of a complex synapse structure

hold tight the damaged organ which

holds tight the measure of attention

lie with a body in the white hush

of a sliding light love the body in its

one life its singular intensity after all

interventions for women

Cambridge, Massachusetts, North Branch and Minneapolis, Minnesota, and Oakland, California, 2019-2020.

I wanted to write a poem about how the industrial food system alienates feminized people from their bodies, and how this alienation requires, colludes with, and exacerbates economic and racial oppressions along with the exploitation of animals. And about how the industrialization of agriculture has been more or less coextensive with the development of modern institutions and technologies for the surveillance and control of the intimate body activities (eating, fucking, reproducing) of women and girls.

While "interventions for women" addresses global food systems and hunger, along with state and NGO approaches to naming systemic failures, its focus is on settler food production and eating in the United States. There is much more to be said about the violence of the food system internationally, not to mention everything else.

I want to say that I intend the title ironically.

○

midway on a journey
through hyper-palatability

something killed
the epithelial cell

little mucosal
microvilli

left me wanting
artificially

enhanced ingredient
experiences

greater than any one
could produce alone

left me not with a barrier
but a hole

O my indeterminate
floating where

have i been
in this sensual body

vague   warm
penetrable

a silver stratus
sheet

a middle-of-the-country
feeling

but of hedonic
eating i.e. consumption

beyond homeostatic
need

i remember quite
everything

even so   it is harder to write
about eating

than sex   depression
or dreaming

strictly from
hunger

appetitive substances
i.e. foods that induce

addictive-like eating   (cake   etc.

growing
harvesting

packing
processing

transforming
marketing

consuming
disposing

a food system encompasses all stages of
keeping us fed

○

food is the single strongest lever
said the EAT-Lancet report

has kept pace with population growth
yet 820 million are hungry

others eat low quality
or too much

be assured #foodcanfixit
so check your planetary health plate

ruled by appetite
i wanted to write

the earthliest
parts of me

wanted to write
against interiority

not of an inside
that gets out

or a boundary

not of a crisis sprung
from pathology

or deficit

instead of the vessel
beyond the periphery

wanted to write
not so much animal as

binding technique
or mucilage

fully organism in the
moment of our glue

in fact the alimentary
canal tube that

begins at the mouth
and ends at the anus

is external to the body
along the way

a wave of slur
enters the throat of the

small bowel
enzymes   bile

bacteria break down
food molecules

aid nutrient
absorption

through the intestinal
wall

into the watery
plasma

and the outside
becomes inside

profound intimacy
of a material world

that is eating
and being eaten

the global challenge
of under- and over-nutrition

the report said a more than
50 percent reduction

in global consumption of foods
like added sugars   red

meat squatting
at the center

will require no less than
a Great Food Transformation

food

available but not present
present but not tasted
tasted but not consumed

please be the beef
please beef she wrote

you can't just walk around
with a hole in yourself

O

feeding 10 billion people
a healthy diet within

safe planetary boundaries
by 2050 is both

possible and necessary
said the EAT-Lancet report

but you know we can make
a hog from a bean

poultry fish milk cows
frying oil and biofuel

from biotech seeds

o

a truth of the whole is
i fell in love

with a girl
in the corn sweat of july

when no one
and everyone

was watching

i wanted to write of that
muggy love

inside of a polemic
about eating

subjects rated cravings
on a scale from

0 (no craving at all) to
100 (strongest craving you've ever experienced of any kind)

"liking" was measured
in a similar manner

into the food swamp
with ravenous maws

○

i started eating because of a
thermal cue

developed feeding behaviors
in the early hours

learned commodity junk-food
inputs like corn

glucose processed into fructose
crystalline   ground   highly pure

in digestion absorbed
directly into the blood

the cult of the nutrient
the cultural carb

monocropped across the tract
of our collective body

golden era of bad food science
and good food capitalism

that was the 1980s

overproduction of the appetitive
my body no different

from the market incentive
a bulk to be sweetened

a monosaccharide sink

wanted the girl
with the most cake

ruled by appetite
i wanted to write

a truth from the
whole

of the scratched-
out line

between what you
call mine

what counts as
your body

and what's a
depository

for Roundup   Teflon
bisphenol A

○

midway
on a journey

through settler
colonial eating

someone used
a surplus

to box-feed
a cow

pierced the floor
with holes

allowing manure
to fall

into a trench
below

harbinger of the
global

animal

the question of what goes
into food

and why   for example
the english

before the regime
when grain fed the poor

noxious additives
alum   bone earth

concealed in dark
brown loaves

produced underground
in holes

then sheep and cattle
bred for fat and meat

broader larger
flesh loads

bones aborted
into bulk

each new field
a machine

into the food swamp
CAFOs

1,000-plus units
equal 1,000 lbs

○

a midwestern childhood is
a cut-up collage

of neighborhood
parks

to tell about those woods
is hard

shirred bandeau tops
in washed-out pinks

ChemLawn knees
hooked over

a scum-slick
trapeze

i don't remember
the park

i remember the feeling
of a park

i don't remember
being watched

i remember the feeling
of being watched

feeling accretes into a
middle-of-the-country

person tough
as a chain people

who enclose
in order to forget

for example
feed-conversion ratios

for example
binge-prone rats

in decades following
developments

in livestock breeding
management

came *l'anorexie hysterique*
in 1873

exhibiting panic when
forced to eat

same year as comstock
in the united states

banning substances
drugs   instruments

designed or intended
to prevent conception

or produce abortion
or for any other purpose

lowd lascivious
indecent immoral

no physiological cause
for lack of appetite

dysfunction of moral
constitution mind

o

i can see our food
on the yellow Formica

canned soups
canned tuna

SPAM   Crisco
Oscar Mayer

what story
do the foods tell

that we were from the
shelf-stable center

of the new right
america

two-job city white
catholic types

whose paychecks
stretched first for

the archdiocese
then groceries

15.6 million food-insecure american households means
15.6 million with difficulty affording enough food to support regular balanced meals

what does it take to make
a kg of beef

15,500 liters of water
20 kg of feed

○

over the new century
american farms

under the new deal
march   rural

reconfiguration
alluvial delta soils

well suited to
appropriation

soybeans   rice
corn   cotton

a farmers home
administration

to deliver blows
in the form of no's

in the form of spittle
from chewing tobacco

to surveil and control
out with plowing

planting   cultivating
picking

in with herbicides
tractors   gmo seeds

fields scrubbed by
usda subsidies

in the south   total
consolidation

accumulation of
white wealth

predicated on
black land theft

from 248 hours
congealed in a bale

to five by the 90s
with help from

chemicals   machines
DDT   toxaphene

biased allotments
debt routines

left the farm
an idle barn

but before the crush
of industry

there was the tuskegee
movable school

buggy on wheels
to teach crop

diversification
terracing pruning

mixing measuring
before cooptation

black women home
demonstration agents

gave lessons in diy
health nutrition

how to raise poultry
make mattresses soap

baby clinics and
birth control

lay midwives
sharecroppers themselves

call it self-defense
call it self-help

mechanization's antidote

o

in which the year-round
sexuality of the human

female was realized to be
the root of our problem

people eating people washing people sleeping people
defecating and urinating

hundreds of millions
will starve

wrote paul ehrlich
in a racist book

called the population bomb
that helped give rise

to the modern
environmental movement

and propel the american
abortion rights campaign

unslackened

we failed to become
a bell-shaped woman

but beneath the liberal
politics of choice

there was lay
gynecology

a counseling service
in everywoman's name

skills maintained
by cadre   or cog   in case

ideal law   a blank
sheet of paper

in the end we can only
rely on each other

in the end a bedroom
can be a bunker

o

no one had ever
touched me

the way i wanted to be
touched

with her i rehearsed
tenderness

my thumb pressed into
the spoon

at the base of
her head

we slept together
in the close heat

metal breeze
through the screen

she kept my secrets
i knew i was

courageous   clean

unsurprisingly   reward
sensitivity

was associated with greater
food addiction symptoms

that the hedonic properties of food   especially food availability   and binge-
eating behavior act as unique mediators

suggest that interventions for reward-sensitive women
may benefit from targeting food availability

a midwestern childhood
is a girl in question

is she a slut   is she
a lesbian

o

we were raised
she and i to be

white and girls

at her house we ate
invert sugar

imitation cheese
detergent emulsifiers

processed SnackWells
devil's food

in front of Lifetime
specials afterschool

didn't know what
any of it was

didn't know anything
about the place

we were from
other than that

it was ours   or so
we were told

but it wasn't

it was
the center of the earth

in dakota   where the
rivers converge

where women
and children

tapped sap
from sugar bush

groves near the water

then pig's eye   fur
stolen goods

cutworms
starving winter

and a war
wooden stockade

camp
in the corridor

and the children
and the women

interned

○

we were pigs
for sure

and none of it
was ours

mostly we smelled like
stolen lip gloss

and the mall
mostly we read tarot

drove aimlessly along
the eerie bluff

above the Nut Goodie
manufacturer

toward the fort
the factory's red

crown   an odd sore
on the valley floor

wide black former
trader path

sang to tapes in a

rusty Cavalier

went home to
what felt like

private fears

a midwestern childhood is
granular   inscrutable

as commodity cropland
milk and cereal

○

said critics of the EAT-
Lancet diet

we would see
in a day

people consuming
just 7g of pork

lamb or beef
the equivalent of

a quarter of a rasher
sixteenth of a burger

half glass of milk
knob of butter

are we talking about
deprivation

destruction
of traditional cuisine

nanny-state
nutritional control

under a plant-based
regime

are we talking about
the right

or the wrong
way to eat

was it infantile desire

restriction-related
hunger

emotional coping or
fear that a core

repulsiveness would be
uncovered

were we clients
unsuitably packaged

for bureaucrats
overdetermined

market factors
for example

every time we sell
ourselves

for example
carbon-intensive meat

no   we learned
in parallel

we could use
and abuse eating

also name
emotional states

meet mutual needs
feed and protect

each other

o

from 20 amino acids
animals plants fungi

build proteins chain
links kinks folds

that an antibody
a blood protein

itself would bind
to a normal protein

is accidental a lapse in
immunological

memory an extra-
intestinal betrayal

like when someone
who loves you

doesn't mean to
hurt you hurts you

you know
ordinary shameful

wanted nothing to cross
the thin membrane

melancholy hole

science of asceticism:

the less you eat drink think love
the greater becomes your treasure

and greater is the store of your
estranged being

o

so it's cake you want
alright

buttercream's
a satin sight

sudden slice
changes the plate

moist to the bite
heavy cream

unbleached flour
work wet   mud texture

into the mound
add butter

over heat   use
a wire

spread to make
a petal flower

eliminate unwanted inflammation and
reverse disease simply by changing
how you eat[!]

into the cakehole
sexual descent

dopamine deluge
creates the impression

of a body
with a surface

euphoric limitation

○

a food system
travels and trades

stunts and wastes
undermines sensitive

value chains
fattens and fails

drives up the cost of
denies access to

nutritious and
sufficient food to

twenty-six percent of the
world's population

with greater insecurity
among women

thus member
agencies advised

nutrition-sensitive
investments

policies for
diversified diets

with reduced
sugars   salt   fats

if possible with
synergies

for sustainability

as each thing to more perfection
grows   said the guide

it feels more sensibly both good
and pain

do you see   if we forgive this
alienated matter of the body

the shadow in the kitchen
the press in impression

we forgive quite everything

○

imagine freedom
from pasturage   surveillance

hunger and thirst
fear and distress

pain   injury   disease

freedom to express
natural behavior

the global right to food

imagine what it would take to
unlearn satisfaction with less

to shatter the
no one and everyone

absolute
power

always and ever
watching

the comings
and goings of girls

drowning effects

Oakland and Point Reyes National Seashore, California, 2016, and Minneapolis, Minnesota, 2020.

I drafted this poem, in part about the effects of climate change in Northern California, before the 2018 Camp Fire, which cost the lives of at least 85 people, and other devastating fires of subsequent years, which have created tremendous hardship. I dedicate this poem to all whose lives have been affected by wildfire.

Throughout, I invoke Emily Dickinson's "My Life had stood – a Loaded Gun" (1863). I also adapt language from reports on the Point Reyes National Seashore Giacomini Wetland Restoration Project along with science writing about ecological thresholds.

last day of the second week
inland forest   midday

heat   meadow brittle
fractured brown   few

sounds at this hour of two

my tongue in diffuse
damp   remains of the burnt-off

fog   read vertical
mixing brings

drier air   first
at the edges   works

toward a center   thicker
Douglas firs

clothed in green lichen

summit of Mt. Wittenberg
dripping

feeling   of falling

absolute warming limits
set   exceeded

active perimeter

a furious red
scrawl   July 22   Soberanes   68,000 acres   50% contained

be READY
harden your home against flying embers

Get SET
prepare your family and home for the possibility of having to evacuate

Be Ready to GO
take evacuation steps necessary to give your family and home the best chance of
surviving a wildfire

bruisy fog   blunts
a mood

tides at two feet
line of white pelicans

from the shore resembles
an overcast

stitch   seam's
raw edge

they thread
the marsh   muck

corral a late-morning
meal

the discussion starts, as all discussions do
in the middle

on one hand   happiness
contentment with

circumstances
a wish   a will   a want

what you want
to have

what we had

timber heat coal light oil speed water corn meat technology
abundantly

how is it that we come to expect so much?

on the other   disappointment

non-fulfillment of expectation
intention   desire

what doesn't turn out to be

a fog around the body
you don't expect to get

lost in   feeling of

dejection   like after

a wreck.   what is a wreck?

          foundered vessel   state of ruin   large heap   abundance
          death of a large number of pelagic birds

debasement
casting down

in geol   matter spewed from
volcanoes

Vesuvian face
most volatile pleasure

          happiness provides
          the emotional setting

          for disappointment

sovereign fantasy

and a mounting sense
of contingency

at first   i roamed
in woods

seemingly *Sovreign*
needing a girl

ponderosa pines'
buttery sap

in my nose   dry
beds   underfoot

needing   a whirl
people said

you're so devoted
loyal   it's

what you are
classed qualifiers

in   June
snow   hard

tight flakes
on a branch   a junco

in clay

all attachment is optimistic

who wants
what they are

at first the project
ponded

during even very
low tides

transitioned from managed
pasture to salt marsh

more rapidly
than expected

the glinting detectable
water table

bright as a promise

similar to natural tidal marshes
in vegetation

species
composition

the promising nature of happiness suggests
happiness lies ahead of us if we

do the right thing

the report said   as marshplains
become vegetated and

hydrolic reworking
slows   the wetland

may play an active role in improving
downstream water quality

a natural buffer against the
drowning effects of sea level rises

in wartime   a farmer

diked the wetland   thought
a wasteland

for milk   made a pasture

Top Tips for Effective Communication About Climate Change Adaptation

1. Balance urgency with hope

limiting warming to 1.5
impossible

                                      at very least, a very difficult task

no avoiding heat waves flooding polar-ice melting coral-reef destruction

                               in the end, I think we just have to hope

i.e. ideally nature
will adapt

and the system will change

                                 on the whole, we like to have hopes
                           they are amongst the things that keep us going

                          some people despair and do not return to hope
                    but many will despair in the hope that hope will return

                 there are times, perhaps, when hope seems to be everything
                    when to give up hope is to plunge into nothingness

and then i simply
unbecame

i was a dark
unfurnished

room   slack
water soundlessly

pooled   still at first
cyanotic

no one saw my body

> *sometimes we desire something so completely that*
> *we revert to our infant selves and scream*

> *in the hope that our desire may be realized*
> *just as, if we were lucky*

> *the milk used to appear in response to our*
> *screams from the cot*

and we will not have

timber heat coal light oil speed water corn meat technology
abundantly

> *Rita   would not drink the milk*
> *from a cup*

from *oikos*
family property house

preserve   happy objects
to preserve   happiness

not at home with   acidification   nine-inch sea level increases   moderate
to very high coastal vulnerability   coastal cliff collapse   etc.

might depend on not being in house

said the report   the so-called
Gradual Continuum Model

which assumes linear changes
from the disturbed condition

does not always hold true

e.g. shorebirds who probe
for prey in marsh

muds   were variable
the winter   after

moderate the second year
rusty sandpipers

droopy gold-speckled

dowitcher   declined
in the third

in fact   species assemblages
may not reach a steady state

instead   the wetland
may evolve over time

in a stage-type fashion
in response to factors

both external and internal

the incapacity to protect loved objects against
external and internal persecutors

is part of the most fundamental
anxiety situation of girls

points where small changes
e.g. how quickly natural channels form

lead to large or discontinuous changes
in other variables

are threshold dynamics

the course of libidinal development is thus
at every step stimulated and reinforced

by the drive for reparation
and ultimately by the sense of guilt

and then i simply
unbecame

i was diffuse   wide

as wind and brine
i was the October boat

weightless whir
no one on the road

heron rookery
in the ficus trees

guano crusting
on the asphalt

farther off   bay
laurel   bluffs

wanted all of it
all of it was enough

80

read seven years into
restoration

spotted California
red-legged frog

threatened by
pesticides   salinity

crimson-bellied
grunting

into the air
water

moved to a marsh

wrote Limantour beach

fogged in   empty of any
hour   some

mornings i wake
thinking

it's spring   this fog's
a throng of

determined ghosts

at the fish dock monitoring site
in the moderate to high

coastal vulnerability area
that summer

pigeon guillemot chicks
hatched and twittered

someone's parent
swooped around the house

to see about all the human
commotion

her legs and feet
a sexual red

streaked the bay's
unpolished silver

like that   she was gone

you were there

Oakland and Point Reyes National Seashore, California, 2017-2018.

I wrote this poem after the April 15, 2017, Berkeley community demonstration against white nationalist and neo-Nazi groups who staged a rally at Martin Luther King Jr. Civic Center Park, and also at the end of the 2011-2017 California drought.

out of the drought
and the dead land

we came undone

cortisol   hypotension
Maalox   adrenaline

beneath a shrill
unblinking cerulean

we're all writing
this poem   i join in

from the train   i eye
the cumulous

vapor   coming off the
cooling towers

against the blue-gray
northeast

blue of a seemingly
thin pellucid

skin   half circling
an eye   it's waste heat

refusal's
a snap back

in the chest   a familiar
too much   not enough

and there was
there is

the tyranny of men
and being left
and despotism

a very bad year   new
body   no new body

at the rally
signs said

hate speech is
free speech

another bad day
under a state that

cares not when
people we love die

reservoir's sudden
swollen state

but no rest
for the water table

cone of depression   soil
collapses   compacts

drops   in fact
an open secret

three sexual
misconduct claims

against the renowned
philosophy professor

that if I showed offense
or refused to comply with

what does it take to
create a hostile environment

what does it take to
uncreate harm

fortunately   depression
and illness

can precipitate
friendship

like inflammation
a protection

the onset of a fight
and it is a fight

guns, race, meat, and manifest destiny
wrote Ruth Ozeki in '98

we are a grisly nation

her question being
can any person eat

any meat   fuck any straight
white men anywhere

under global capitalist
patriarchy

and not be made
sick   and i think

her answer is
well   no

someone i love said
it wasn't all bad

and i said   no
certainly there was

beauty   but what
was it   and when

will i think of it
and feel something

other than a blow

and friends litanize
a new set of imperatives

we must shut down
the airports now

we must shut down
the fascist rallies now

we must become
anonymous

the truth is not
new   but still

mostly very
difficult to face

and we cross over
a threshold

into something like
the evental

or a vignetted dream
in its process of

emptying out

a residue on your
skin   a damp

that attests   it happened
you were there

going with that
for awhile

she touches me
very lightly

my body tilts
toward her

a sudden wire
hold my breath

want everything to
have been different

sharper   clarifying as
this absolute desire

early fog clings like a tone
called stay

everything stretched
as in a memory

your frightening body
distorted by the surface

wan   a pool
isn't peace   or pace   no

the widening life

between what's
been left and what

doesn't yet matter
but will

i'm tired of cruelty
angrier than i let

myself admit
someone i love said

wake up   take stock
don't forget

on the peninsula
gray tank

no line in the vaporous
air   pelican

gyre   effortless
dip   cut in the wet

thick   what's
without weight   scarlet

lids   fog   bath
today   pain

in my head
concepts

slow   what
hurts   prairie's

bend   or burst
in the chest

cavity of the gull
eldrin   or blubber

abrasion   or coastal
collapse

what hurts
what can't

get up   or out
or into

elephant seals in their species
being   being

sputtering
like the old motor   water

caught in a drain   bawdily
to an admiring colony

do they wake up   think
here i am   here

is some food   sex
here is a fight   needs

more or less
naked as my own

and the air   a door   gulls
chattering   whimpering

scratching at it to be
let in

what is the question
what matters

what is poetry but
a bloc

a collective self-
defense act   there is

one thing and it
is only one thing

no one can take away your
description of what is lived

meat habitats

Oakland, California, and Minneapolis, Minnesota, 2017-2019.

I started writing this poem just under a year after the 2016 election, alongside many others who were also trying to write about surviving sexual violence.

A maltreated animal
can be borne by no one
except almost everyone
— Evelyn Reilly

flattened cells   a tight
weave

clutch the organism   form
a protein envelope

self-regulating
environment

more or less stable victory
in the unlikely history

of something
and not nothing

we go out   invade

plant and animal
cellular structures

restrict water flow

assemble harm

pathologize need

things we never should

and relationships feel
increasingly unmanageable

and power wants into
the hollow

distinct nuclei
clot   bean-sized

behind the eyes
controls

hunger
thirst
attachment behaviors
emotions
memory

congealed   holds
vertebrates

captive   circadian

triggers death events
in 3 x 5 cm pyramidal

semilunar or crescent-shaped
fat capsules

below the diaphragm

from cholesterol   the body makes
steroid hormones

that rush the heart arms legs
turn blood thick and sweet

it's dealing
with an emergency

long-term activation linked to

digestive problems
headaches
heart disease
sleep problems
weight gain
memory and concentration impairment

(what do i know about
the inside of your body

after the election the hate site said

we want them to feel that everything around them is against them
and we want them to be afraid

concerns about the possibility of sudden deportation
forced separation
linked to increased symptoms of anxiety and depression

lesbian gay and bisexual people in communities with high levels of
antigay prejudice had a risk of death
three times higher

what is the number
for trans women of color?

increased incidents of harassment   hateful intimidation
most commonly reported at k12 schools

may we always be
the power of our persistence and fury

may we always be
against the law

full stop.   october orange
in the artery   congested

river   whey
in the tanker trucks

along the bald
interstate exit

ethanol corridor
are you fuel

flexible?   if you like
fill up   on corn

a place
will make you

sick
and young

the proposal:

fabrication of 3D printed extruded pig cells to form
real organic dwellings

a victimless shelter

are you getting enough?

globular protein
mixture

projected to reach a value over
$75,952 million

are you getting enough?

byproduct   separated
from the fatty

coagulation

a value-added whey
pool

driven by
positive consumer

perception

giving a sweet milky
taste to your

preparations

and i see violence
everywhere

a fraction of the size of a human hair

i see violence
on your   nails wrists teeth and gums

a place
will make you

white
and sure

allegedly

allegedly kissed
allegedly exposed
allegedly offered
allegedly asked
allegedly grabbed
allegedly groped
allegedly summoned
allegedly moved
allegedly pushed
allegedly pulled
allegedly propositioned
allegedly badgered
allegedly discarded
allegedly climbed
allegedly forced
allegedly tried
allegedly masturbated
allegedly raped
allegedly warned

aggressively
repeatedly
pushed

from behind

repeatedly
offered

*believed he was going
to rape me*

*accidentally
kill me*

effective and less
costly   whey

concentrates in

ready-to-use
therapeutic

foods can be
assessed by asking the

mother to sit
quietly with the child

in dreams the violence
is ridiculous

knives through
the hardboard

into my hands
flattened against it

a hook   shock
in the cortisol

night   sign
over a door

in riotous green
neon blinked

freedom   inside
blood   acts   sounds

collapses
into acquiescence

woke up to the stun
of a body intact

you thought your body
was your own

but a body is not a boundary
a door is not a dam

no sentient being
was harmed in

laboratory growth
of the skin

i worry so much
about you

i worry you won't
get enough air

that you'll
run into the street

fuck someone
unkind

suffer

searched *i worry so much
about you*

first return *'i am so worried about you. are you okay? you scared me.'* what is it
with women who constantly say this type of stuff?

an ultra-processed
elixir

requiring no health
authority figure

in my loneliness
the flood of oxytocin

nearly incapacitates me

understand the effects of social
hostility on health

in order to facilitate effective
coping and resilience

the perfect basic ingredients
to produce

an optimal formula
closest to breast milk

a place
will make

your body
a warning

sodium benzoate   preservative to kill
yeasts bacteria fungi

other materials include
collagen powder
xanthan gum
mannitol
cochineal
sodium pyrophosphate
and recycled PET

plastic scaffold

suitable for both
food and feed

at $15 per hundredweight
the system incentivizes

farmers to produce more
and more milk

overproduction
weighs

causing some to sell
or slaughter

to make herds
smaller

some process manure
in tanks

called digesters   turn methane
to power

once the fears included   gum in a man's mouth hair above a man's lip
silhouette of a neighbor cut into a curtain warts needles shit hands growing
breasts and hair sirens and basements gas leaks and fires my mother's
bleeding carcasses in the leaves running out of food hugging my sister too
hard accidents kidnappings suffocation poison

(when is a harm
done

(when is a harm
a slanted one

survivors reported chronic
anxiety tension phobias

feelings of confusion disorientation
difficulty experiencing feelings

the feeling that one should forget

(what does it mean to
experience feelings

(what does it mean to forget

he said   there is a drain.
find it.

you thought you could peer out
from the safety of your

private   electric
pulp

idea-like memory-like picture-like or song-like

fears include running out of money   running out of
water   losing someone you love

more than you   love yourself

and relationships feel
increasingly unmanageable

everyone is someone who has hurt you or
someone who has protected someone who has hurt you

(and you are someone who has protected someone
who has hurt someone too

the concept model consists of very expensive
fitted cured pork or

articulated swine leather with an
extensive shelf life

a non-perishable 11 x 3 x 7 in
prototype

i would like to say
i would like for you to say to me

help me understand how not to become someone
who protects someone who has hurt you

it's beautiful   she wrote   with parts i can
relate to

people everywhere
are sick

and i am not writing poems
i am barely moving at all

will we   as we have
refuse

sober consideration
civil discourse

proportion
diagnoses and cures

will we demand
disobedience

speak from the raw
center of a wound

lock eyes
with a friend's

across the room
to form a spine

when the room
can't hold you

love is a cord and
all love is political

say no

Minneapolis, Minnesota, and San Francisco, California, 2020.

I started writing this poem during the COVID-19 pandemic, several months after the May 25, 2020 murder of George Floyd, a Black man, by the white police officer Derek Chauvin along with the Minneapolis Police Department; after the dismantling of the summer sanctuary camp at Powderhorn Park by the City of Minneapolis; and during the catastrophic late-summer and early-fall wildfires in California, Oregon, and Washington.

the streets are young and vital
as ever

we owe a debt
the night

wet in the sick
dusk   every history

grips a crowd
conscious or not

in its fist

conscious or not

of the known world
simply gone

(go into the poem
the crowd

the riot   knowing
what you are

your daily   deadly
potential

comrade
conspirator
sibling
lover

whatever you are
you're no less lethal

liberalism's
machinery

a sudden   splitting
force

chemical agent's
a neighbor

naked in its
collusion course

any neighbor
a cop

any discourse
a *modality of the police*

(what would it take to
say no to

withholding's
economy

there was the adrenaline
of the refuge

in the heat
in the park

donation needs
included

. . . .
oral pain relief
cigarettes
28 & 29-gauge syringes
sharps containers
contact solution
emergency blankets
sleeping mats
towels
sleeping bags
sweatpants
. . . .

despite predictable
evictions

praxes of
provision

. . . .
new xl tshirts
duct tape
lanterns
pillows & cases

battery-powered fans
compression bandages
phone chargers
hand sanitizer
pop
. . . .

what we need is
something beyond

prescribed models
of what they

recognize as care

contagion time's
a time for choosing

clarifying acts of love
and refusing

vermilion august
pummels thinner

distant branches
vessels leak

a white opacity
clots land in a lung

below sticky
water molecules

move with capillary
tubes   drag hundreds

of gallons up each
coastal redwood

root systems
extend a hundred

feet   entwine with
roots of others

even a downed tree
can survive

into our lungs
ash of accumulated

fuel loads   forest
homes

where we'd loved
each other's body

generously
under the canopy

on the spicy floor

after the lightning
surfaces of home

bathed in gold
the sky splashed

with corals
tens of thousands

ordered to go

before the month
mark

light went out
of the sky

noon was a
shallow dish

of ash
translucent

orange
glass turned

upside down

*you cannot think your way
out of the problem*

you've got to use fire

on the porch
in the heat

at a distance of
six feet

i said i'm
in your hands

she said   it's sweet
isn't it

my bark thickens
with every year now

i keep your words
in my ear now

all i want is to touch you

tell me again what you did

notes

interventions for women

On a few occasions, I invoke Dante Alighieri's *Inferno*.

I wrote this poem after moving back to Minnesota, the place of my birth and indoctrination into Christian settler white supremacy. I was raised on stolen Dakota land, near the sacred Bdote, where the Haha Wakpa, or Mississippi river, and Mnisota Wakpa, or Minnesota river, converge. At one point, in my mother's kitchen, I came across the *Nativity Heritage Cookbook* (1980), authored by my childhood parish's Council of Catholic Women. As its preface, the cookbook features a reproduction of a handwritten 1922 settler manifesto from the archbishop to a new priest, describing the geographic area of the new parish, sited not far from Bdote. The archbishop describes it as a "very large territory," "a field that will demand hard and constant labor." The letter is signed "Sincerely Yours in Christ." In this way, the settler family's feminized labor of preparing "Grandpa's Meat Loaf" or "Ham Towers" is tacitly framed as a form of meaningful participation in the inherited project of Christian settlement and Indigenous erasure. Among other things, "interventions for women" is an attempt to confront my own settler colonial eating, from the place where I learned to eat.

Sources referenced or adapted, in order of appearance:

Lorine Niedecker. "Paean to Place." *Collected Works*. University of California Press, 2002.

Natalie J. Loxton and Renee J. Tipman. "Reward sensitivity and food addiction in women." *Appetite*, vol. 115, 2017.

Committee on World Food Security. *www.fao.org/cfs*. The Committee on World Food Security is an "intergovernmental platform" that reports to the UN.

The EAT-Lancet Commission. "Summary Report of the EAT-Lancet Commission: Healthy Diets from Sustainable Food Systems." *Eatforum.org*, 2019. The EAT-Lancet Commission is a "global, non-profit startup."

EAT-Lancet Commission. "Summary Report."

Loxton and Tipman. "Reward sensitivity."

Gertrude Stein. "Roast Beef." *Tender Buttons*, 1914.

"Courtney Love Barbara Walters Interview," 1995.

EAT-Lancet Commission. "Summary Report."

USDA. "USDA Coexistence Fact Sheets: Soybeans." *www.usda.gov*, 2015.

Sarah E. Polk, et al. "Wanting and liking: Separable components in problematic eating behavior?" *Appetite*, vol. 115, 2017.

Varsha Tiwari, et al. "Role of breast crawl in maternal health and wellbeing." *International Journal of Medical Research and Review*, vol. 3, no. 6, 2015.

Michael Pollan. "Unhappy Meals." *New York Times Magazine*, January 28, 2007.

John Bellamy Foster. "Marx as a Food Theorist." *Monthly Review*, December 2016.

Ernest-Charles Lasègue. "On hysterical anorexia" (1873). *Evolution of Psychosomatic Concepts: Anorexia Nervosa, a Paradigm*, ed. Ralph M. Kaufman and Marcel Heiman. International Universities Press, 1964.

For a brief overview of the Comstock Act, see "Anthony Comstock's 'Chastity' Laws" at www.pbs.org.

Lasègue. "On hysterical anorexia."

Alisha Coleman-Jensen, et al. "Household Food Security in the United States in 2016." *USDA Economic Research Report*, no. 237, September 2017.

Vann R. Newkirk II. "The Great Land Robbery." *The Atlantic*, September 2019.

Pete Daniel. *Dispossession: Discrimination Against African American Farmers in the Age of Civil Rights*. University of North Carolina Press, 2013.

Susan L. Smith. *Sick and Tired of Being Sick and Tired: Black Women's Health Activism in America, 1890-1950*. University of Pennsylvania Press, 1995.

Paul Ehrlich. *The Population Bomb*. Buccaneer Books, 1968.

Thomas Robertson. *The Malthusian Moment: Global Population Growth and the Birth of American Environmentalism*. Rutgers University Press, 2012.

Laura Kaplan. *The Story of Jane: The Legendary Underground Feminist Abortion Service*. Pantheon Books, 1995.

Loxton and Tipman. "Reward sensitivity."

Gary Clayton Anderson and Alan Woolworth, eds. *Through Dakota Eyes: Narrative Accounts of the Minnesota Indian War of 1862*. Minnesota Historical Society Press, 1988.

Ingrid Torjesen. "WHO pulls support from initiative promoting global move to plant based foods." *British Medical Journal*, no. 365, April 2019.

Grace Rasmusson, et al. "Household food insecurity is associated with binge-eating disorder and obesity." *International Journal of Eating Disorders*, no. 52, November 2018.

Rebecca J. Lester. *Famished: Eating Disorders and Failed Care in America*. University of California Press, 2019.

Sarah Ballantyne. *The Paleo Approach: Reverse Autoimmune Disease and Heal Your Body*. Victory Belt Publishing, 2014.

Karl Marx. "Human Requirements and Division of Labour Under the Rule of Private Property." *Economic & Philosophic Manuscripts of 1844*.

Sarah Ballantyne. *thepaleomom.com*.

FAO, IFAD, UNICEF, WFP, and WHO. *The State of Food Security and Nutrition in the World 2020: Transforming food systems for affordable healthy diets.* Rome, FAO, 2020. https://doi.org/10.4060/ca9692en. The FAO, IFAD, UNICEF, WFP and WHO are multi-state agencies under the UN.

Sara Ahmed. *The Cultural Politics of Emotion.* Routledge, 2004.

Heather McLeod-Kilmurray. "Does the Rule of Ecological Law Demand Veganism? Ecological Law, Interspecies Justice, and the Global Food System." *Vermont Law Review*, vol. 43, no. 455, 2019.

Lester. *Famished.*

drowning effects

Throughout, I adapt language from:

Lorraine Parsons and Amelia Ryan. "Year Five of the Giacomini Wetland Restoration Project: Analysis of Changes in Physical and Ecological Conditions in the Project Area." Point Reyes National Seashore, National Park Service, 2015.

Giacomini Wetland Restoration Project website.

Elizabeth G. King and Steven Whisenant. "Thresholds in Ecological and Linked Social-Ecological Systems: Application to Restoration." *New Models for Ecosystem Dynamics and Restoration*, ed. Richard J. Hobbs, Katharine N. Suding, and Society for Ecological Restoration International. Island Press, 2008.

Sources quoted (in italics), in order of appearance:

Cal Fire "Ready, Set, Go! Campaign." *www.readyforwildfire.org.*

Lauren Berlant and Lee Edelman. *Sex, or the Unbearable.* Duke University Press, 2014.

Sara Ahmed. *The Promise of Happiness.* Duke University Press, 2010.

"wreck, n." *OED Online*.

Ahmed. *Promise of Happiness*.

Climate expert Peter Wadhams. Presentation. Point Reyes National
Seashore, 2016.

Marine ecologist Ben Becker. Presentation. Point Reyes National Seashore,
2016.

Ian Craib. *The Importance of Disappointment*. Routledge, 1994.

Melanie Klein. *Love, Guilt, and Reparation: And Other Works 1921-1945*. The
Free Press, 1975.

Ahmed. *The Promise of Happiness*.

Klein. *Love, Guilt, and Reparation*.

you were there

At one point, I reference Ruth Ozeki's *My Year of Meats*, Penguin, 1999.

meat habitats

My epigraph is from Evelyn Reilly, "Moo," in *Echolocation*, Roof Books, 2018.

Some language in this poem is adapted from accounts of sex crimes
committed by Harvey Weinstein and also Christine Blasey Ford's account
of being sexually assaulted by Brett Kavanaugh; an article by D.R. Williams
and M.M. Medlock titled "Health Effects of Dramatic Societal Events —
Ramifications of the Recent Presidential Election" in *New England Journal
of Medicine*, vol. 376, no. 23, 2017; a statement by Mara Keisling and
the National Center for Transgender Equality in response to the federal
government's 2018 proposal to define gender as a biological, immutable
condition determined at birth and, thus, to eliminate the civil rights of
trans people; various reports on dairy and global whey protein markets; and

language describing a project of Terreform ONE, a nonprofit architecture and urban design research group.

Terreform ONE "endeavor[s] to combat the extinction of planetary species through pioneering acts of design." I came across Terreform ONE's project "In Vitro Meat Habitat" as I was beginning to work on this poem. They write that the "In Vitro Meat Habitat" is "an architectural proposal for the fabrication of 3D printed extruded pig cells to form real organic dwellings. It is intended to be a 'victimless shelter,' because no sentient being was harmed in the laboratory growth of the skin. We used sodium benzoate as a preservative to kill yeasts, bacteria and fungi. Other materials in the model matrix are: collagen powder, xanthan gum, mannitol, cochineal, sodium pyrophosphate, and recycled PET plastic scaffold. As of now, the concept model consists of essentially very expensive fitted cured pork or articulated swine leather with an extensive shelf life. The actual scale of the non-perishable prototype is 11 in x 3 in x 7 in."
See https://terreform.org/in-vitro-meat-habitat.

say no

Sources quoted, referenced, or adapted, in order of appearance:

T.J. Tallie. "Asymptomatic Lethality: Cooper, COVID-19, and the Potential for Black Death." *Nursing Clio*, June 8, 2020.

Idris Robinson. "How It Might Should Be Done." Lecture delivered July 20, 2020.

Statement by Minneapolis Sanctuary Camp activist and resident. The Minneapolis Sanctuary Movement began at a Sheraton in South Minneapolis during the uprisings following George Floyd's murder. For nearly two weeks, unsheltered people had access to safe, free housing at the hotel. When residents were suddenly evicted, some decided to set up a camp at Powderhorn Park. Community members supported the camp by organizing supply donations, meals, first aid, and harm-reduction support. In June, the Minneapolis park board named parks sanctuaries for unhoused people, a win for the Sanctuary Movement. But then in July, under pressure from local homeowners, the park board and the Minneapolis Police

Department began evicting people. By the middle of August, the city had evicted all remaining residents of Powderhorn Park.

Elizabeth Shogren. "A Century of Fire Suppression Is Why California Is in Flames." *Mother Jones*, December 12, 2017.

acknowledgements

This book, about and indebted to place, was written on Dakota, Coast Miwok, Massachusett, Ohlone, and Ojibwe ancestral and contemporary lands.

Thank you to Mitchell Joachim and Terreform ONE for permission to include an image of the "In Vitro Meat Habitat" on the cover of this book.

Thank you to Mary Newell, Bernard Quetchenbach, and Sarah Nolan for publishing "may the human animals" in *Poetics for the More-than-Human World: An Anthology of Poetry & Commentary* (Spuyten Duyvil, 2020) and to Brenda Iijima for publishing an early hand-written version of the poem in *Guest: a journal of guest editors* 2.

Thank you to Robert Hass for nominating me for the 2016 Climate Change at the Western Edge Residency, held jointly by the Mesa Refuge and the Point Reyes National Seashore Association. While in residence, I wrote a first draft of "drowning effects." Thank you to Jamie Townsend and Nicholas DeBoer for publishing "you were there" in *Elderly* 29. All my gratitude to MC Hyland, Anna Gurton-Wachter, and Jeff Peterson of DoubleCross Press for publishing "meat habitats" as a chapbook in 2019. My deepest thanks to Gillian Hamel, Rusty Morrison, Ken Keegan, Kayla Ellenbecker, and everyone at Omnidawn for their continued support of my work.

Thank you to the people who read or listened to drafts of these poems; shared words, knowledge, and brilliance; fed and housed me during my writing and editing process; and/or offered friendship, care, and kinship—all of which helped me think and grow and make this book what it is: Darrell Alvarez, Priyanka Basu, Drew Belstock, Mei-mei Berssenbrugge, Chris Chen, Linci Comy, Charise DeBerry, Paul Ebenkamp, Julie Eckerle, Farivar family, Merle Geode, Judy Grahn, Richard Hernandez, Brenda Hillman, Brenda Iijima, Kate Jalma, Elliot James, Lynn Keller, Kitses family, Michael Kleber-Diggs, Vanessa McKinney, Rachel Moritz, G.E. Patterson, Thane Plantikow, Samia Rahimtoola, Evelyn Reilly, Joan Retallack, Frances Richard, Steve Rowell, Jocelyn Saidenberg, Lysa Samuel, Eric Sneathen, Laura Woltag, Noelle Yackel, Stephanie Young. Thank you to Evelyn, Eric, and Stephanie for reading and responding to the full manuscript in draft form. Thank you to my family.

author bio

Angela Hume is the author of the full-length poetry book *Middle Time* (Omnidawn, 2016). Her chapbooks include *Meat Habitats* (DoubleCross, 2019), *Melos* (Projective Industries, 2015), *The Middle* (Omnidawn, 2013), and *Second Story of Your Body* (Portable Press at Yo-Yo Labs, 2011). With Gillian Osborne, she co-edited *Ecopoetics: Essays in the Field* (University of Iowa Press, 2018). Angela is at work on a nonfiction book about the feminist self-help movement in the Bay Area (AK Press, 2023).

Interventions for Women
Angela Hume

Cover image credit: "In Vitro Meat Habitat." Mitchell Joachim, Terreform ONE.

Text set in Electra LT Std

Cover design by adam b. bohannon

Printed in the United States
by Books International, Dulles, Virginia
On Glatfelter 50# Cream Natures Book 440 ppi
Acid Free Archival Quality Recycled Paper

Publication of this book was made possible in part by gifts from
Katherine & John Gravendyk in honor of Hillary Gravendyk,
Francesca Bell, Mary Mackey, and The New Place Fund

Omnidawn Publishing
Oakland, California
Staff and Volunteers, Fall 2021

Rusty Morrison & Ken Keegan, senior editors & co-publishers
Kayla Ellenbecker, production editor & poetry editor
Gillian Olivia Blythe Hamel, senior editor & book designer
Trisha Peck, senior editor & book designer
Rob Hendricks, editor for *Omniverse*, marketing, fiction & post-pub publicity
Sharon Zetter, poetry editor & book designer
Liza Flum, poetry editor
Matthew Bowie, poetry editor
Anthony Cody, poetry editor
Jason Bayani, poetry editor
Gail Aronson, fiction editor
Laura Joakimson, marketing assistant for Instagram & Facebook, fiction editor
Ariana Nevarez, marketing assistant & Omniveres writer, fiction editor
Jennifer Metsker, marketing assistant